Good People Everywhere

Cynthia Harmony, M.A.

We all have a super power.

We can help people and the world!

I clean up trash.

I give my pet food.

I carry bags from the market.

Think and Talk

How do you help at home?

I pet my dog.

I feed my brother.

We plant trees.

I share my umbrella.

We call our family.

I help my sister ride.

We help baby turtles.

We share our candy.

We wait our turn.

How do you use your super power?

Jump into Fiction

Maya Waves

Maya loves walks with her grandma.

They wave and say hello.

One smile turns into two.

Joy is all around.

Café
31

Civics in Action

People show kindness every day. They help. They share. They care.

1. Think about someone who has been kind.

2. What did they do?

3. Make them an award! Give it to them.